1 potato 2 potato
and 165 TASTY TATER TREATS more!

By
Brenda O'Connell Ledridge

Published By
Edw. D. Donahoe, Publishers
P. O. Box 22011
Louisville, Kentucky 40222
ISBN 0-933400-03-7

Being a good ol' Irish country girl whose ancestry dates back to a poor Irish potato farmer in the early 1800's, it was only natural that I would partake of the potato once a day — like a daily vitamin.

My grandmothers served potatoes for breakfast, lunch, and dinner, seven days a week in some fashion or another.

My doctors, all six of them, screamed, "You must eat a potato a day to keep the iron deficiency away" while I was awaiting the birth of each of my three children.

The crowning blow came one evening at dinner when my husband sat down to his 365th baked potato and said, "I'm sick of baked potatoes. Can't you think of some other ways to fix them if we are going to have them so often?"

So, with the help of my children, I gathered up pen and pad and set out to gather all the possible ways to prepare potatoes. Thus we compiled the recipes you will find in this cookbook.

I was planning to publish and distribute the book locally until I ran across some of the cookbooks published by Edward Donahoe Publishing Company in the finer bookstores. I liked his books, dropped him a line to tell him what I had "cooked up," he liked it, and thus you have *Tasty Tater Treats.*

Dedicated to Roger, Aimee and Ryan

Copyright 1980, Brenda O'Connell Ledridge

Main Dish Potatoes

Potatoes cooked with Beef, Ham, Hot dogs, Sausage, Pork Chops, Shrimp, Scallops, Tuna, Fish, and Chicken — including Stews, Hash, Pizza, Tacos

POTATO MEAT ROLL

1½ pounds hamburger
2 eggs
½ cup bread crumbs
1 medium onion, minced

½ can creamed mushroom soup
2 cups mashed potatoes
1 t. salt
½ t. pepper

Combine hamburger, bread crumbs, one beaten egg, salt, onion, and pepper. Shape into a rectangle on waxed paper. Mix together soup, potatoes, and remaining egg, beaten. Place this on top of meat and roll like a jelly roll. Bake at 350 degrees for 1 hour.

POTATO-CHEESEBURGER CASSEROLE

1 pound ground beef
1 small onion, diced
Dash of salt and pepper
1 16-ounce can corn, drained

1 cup shredded cheese
½ cup catsup
1 egg, beaten
1 cup mashed potatoes

Brown beef and onion in shortening and drain. Add salt, pepper, corn, cheese and catsup and mix together well. Spoon into a greased casserole dish. Mix together the egg and potatoes and smooth over meat mixture. Bake at 350 degrees for 30 minutes.

HAMBURGER-POTATO PIE

1 medium onion, chopped
1 pound ground beef
1 teaspoon salt
½ teaspoon pepper
1 can lima beans or green beans (drained)

1 can tomato juice or sauce
5 medium potatoes, boiled
½ cup milk
1 egg

Brown onion and beef in shortening and drain. Add salt and pepper, beans and tomato sauce and stir. Pour into a greased baking dish. Mash potatoes with milk, egg, and dash of salt and pepper. Spoon over beef mixture. Bake at 350 degrees for 30 minutes.

POTATO-HAM MOLD

1 envelope unflavored gelatin
1½ cup chicken broth
2 T. dry mustard
3 T. sweet pickle relish
2 T. green pepper, diced
1 small onion, diced

1 T. sugar
1 stalk celery, chopped fine
2 cups chopped, cooked potatoes
2 cups chopped, baked ham
½ cup mayonnaise
4 hard-boiled eggs, chopped

Heat chicken broth. Add gelatin and stir to dissolve. Set aside. Mix together remaining ingredients and toss gently. Add broth-gelatin to hamburger-potato mixture and turn into a mold that has been lightly oiled. Chill for several hours until firm.

BAKED HAM AND POTATOES

2 pounds of sliced smoked ham
4-6 medium potatoes, sliced
2 medium onions, sliced

½ cup flour
Dash of salt and pepper

Place ham slice in roasting pan. Add layer of potatoes and onions. Sift flour over this and add enough milk to half cover the ingredients. Sprinkle with a dash of salt and pepper. Cover and bake at 350 degrees for 1 hour.

BAKED HOT DOG-WEINERS

3 T. butter
3 T. flour
1 t. salt
1 t. dry mustard
Dash of pepper
1 cup milk
1 cup buttered bread crumbs

1 cup mayonnaise
4 medium potatoes, cooked & cubed
1 can cut green beans, drained
1 small onion, diced
½ cup chopped pimientos
1 pound weiners, boiled & sliced

Melt butter in sauce pan over low heat. Stir in flour, salt, mustard, and pepper until blended. Add milk gradually until sauce is thick and bubbly. Remove from heat and add mayonnaise until blended. Stir in the potatoes, green beans, onion, pimientos, and weiners. Spoon into greased baking dish. Sprinkle with bread crumbs. Bake at 350 degrees for 30-40 minutes.

POTATO STEW

1 pound ground beef
1 large onion, diced
3 carrots, diced
3 medium raw potatoes, cubed
1 green pepper, diced

1 8 ounce can tomato sauce
1 t. salt
Dash of pepper
2 bouillon cubes

Roll ground beef into small balls. Salt and pepper. Brown in grease. Add 3 cups water, onion, carrots, potatoes, green pepper, tomato sauce, salt, pepper and bouillon cubes. Simmer until meat is cooked and sauce reaches desired thickness.

BAKED POTATO STEW

2 T. bacon grease
1 cup sliced onion
1 pound ground beef
½ cup uncooked rice
3 cups diced raw potatoes
1 cup diced celery
1 can kidney beans

1 t. salt
¼ t. pepper
½ t. chili powder
Dash of Worcestershire sauce
1 can tomato sauce
½ cup water

Pour 2 T. bacon grease into deep casserole dish. Arrange onion slices, ground beef, rice, potatoes, celery and beans in layers. Combine seasoning, tomato sauce, and water and pour over meat and vegetables. Cover and bake in a 325 degree oven for 2½-3 hours.

MEAT BALLS AND POTATOES

1 pound ground beef
1 cup bread crumbs
1 egg, well beaten
1 T. minced onion
1 t. salt
¼ t. pepper

¼ cup flour
2 cups canned tomatoes
2 cups diced potatoes
1 cup carrots, diced
1 cup minced onion
1 cup celery, diced

Mix together first six ingredients and roll into small balls. Roll balls in flour and brown in shortening. Put balls into greased casserole dish. Stir together remaining five ingredients and add another teaspoon of salt. Pour this over the meat balls. Cover and bake at 350 degress for 1 hour.

SAUSAGE AND POTATOES

8 smoked sausage links
1 small jar cheese spread
1 cup sour cream

1 small onion, minced
1 t. salt
6 medium potatoes, cooked & sliced

Mix together cheese spread and sour cream. Add onion and salt. Blend until smooth. Add sliced potatoes, and sausage links sliced. Put in greased casserole dish and bake at 350 degrees for 45 minutes.

HAM-POTATO HASH

1-2 cups chopped ham
4-6 medium cooked, cubed potatoes
1 onion, sliced

6 strips bacon
Dash of salt & pepper

Fry bacon until crisp and remove from grease. Saute' onions in bacon grease. Add ham and potatoes to onions. Dust with flour, salt and pepper and stir. Add enough milk to make a thickened sauce. Simmer until heated thoroughly. Serve on toast or biscuits garnished with bacon crumbs.

SWEET POTATO-PORK CHOP CASSEROLE

Cook 2-3 large sweet potatoes in jackets. Remove skin and cool. Cut in halves lengthwise. Brown 4-6 pork chops and season with salt & pepper.

Combine 2 T. cornstarch, 2 T. brown sugar, and the juice from 1 can sliced pineapple. Cook juice for 10 minutes.

Arrange pork chops in baking dish. Place one pineapple slice and one sweet potato half on top of each pork chop. Pour juice over and bake at 300 degrees until potatoes are glazed.

PORK CHOPS-POTATO CASSEROLE

4 pork chops, browned
2 cups sliced potatoes
Salt & pepper

1 medium onion, sliced
1 can cream of mushroom soup

Place potatoes in greased casserole dish. Season with salt & pepper. Arrange onion slices on top and pour on mushroom soup. Repeat layers again. Finish with pork chops and cover. Bake 1 hour at 350 degrees.

POTATOES AND CHOPS

4 chops (pork, veal, or lamb)
4 potatoes, sliced
1 cup sour cream

1 cup minced onions
1 t. salt
Dash pepper

Brown chops in grease and arrange in baking dish. Put layer of potatoes and onions onto chops and pour sour cream over all. Sprinkle with salt and pepper. Cover and bake at 350 degrees for 1 hour.

FISH BALLS

Combine mashed potatoes with any flaked fish and 1 beaten egg. Roll in flour. Season with salt and pepper and fry in vegetable oil until brown.

SHRIMP POTATOES

4-5 potatoes
¼ cup butter
1 can cream of shrimp soup

¼ t. salt
⅛ t. pepper
Shredded cheddar cheese

Bake potatoes until completely done. Cool potatoes and cut in half. Scoop out pulp and mash. Combine with butter, soup, salt and pepper and mix well. Stuff potato mixture into potato shell. Sprinkle with cheese. Place on baking sheet and bake about 10 minutes until cheese is melted.

SCALLOPS-POTATOES

8 medium potatoes
1¼ cups dry white wine
1 pound scallops
½ cup water

1 cup mayonnaise
2 T. lemon juice
½ t. salt
¼ t. pepper

Cook potatoes until tender. Cool and peel. Cut into cubes and pour one-half of the wine over the potatoes. Boil the scallops in the remaining wine and water for about 7 minutes. Drain and cool. Mix together the mayonnaise, lemon juice, salt and pepper. Toss together the potatoes and scallops. Add enough of the mayonnaise mixture to desired taste. Can be served warm or cold.

POTATO-TUNA PIE

1 cup mayonnaise
1 small onion grated
2 t. lemon juice
1 t. Worcestershire sauce
1 t. salt

2 cans drained tuna fish (7 oz. each)
1 pkg. frozen mixed vegetables, thawed
½ cup chopped celery
2 cups mashed potatoes

Stir together 3/4 cup mayonnaise and the next 7 ingredients. Put into greased pie plate and bake at 350 degrees for 15 minutes. Stir together potatoes and 1/4 cup mayonnaise. Spread layer of potatoes over top of pie. Broil in oven until lightly brown.

TATERS AND FISH

1 egg, separated
2 T. melted butter
1 cup flour
1 t. salt

1 cup buttermilk
5-6 medium potatoes
2 pounds boned fish

Combine egg yolk, butter, flour, salt and buttermilk to make batter for fish. Beat until smooth. Beat egg white until stiff. Fold into the batter. Wash and peel potatoes. Cut into the desired size strips and leave in cold water until ready to fry. Wash fish in cold salted water and pat dry. Pour 3-4 inches vegetable oil into pan. Drain the potatoes and drop into hot oil. Fry potatoes until golden brown. Drain on paper towel. Dip the fish into the batter and fry a few pieces at a time until browned. Drain on paper towel. Place chips and fish on a large platter. Sprinkle with salt, and serve warm.

SKILLET STEAK AND POTATOES

1½ pounds boneless round steak
¼ cup flour
2 t. salt
¼ t. pepper
2 T. vegetable oil

1 can beef broth
1 cup water
4 medium potatoes, peeled and sliced
2 medium onions, chopped

Cut meat into bit-sized pieces. Combine flour, salt and pepper. Dredge steak in flour mixture and brown in oil. Add broth and water, cover and simmer for 30-40 minutes. Turn meat and top with potatoes and onion. Cover and simmer 30 minutes longer.

NEW ENGLAND BEEF AND POTATOES

3 pounds boneless beef round rump roast
2 cans onion soup
1 T. horseradish
1 t. garlic salt
6 carrots, chopped

8 small whole potatoes
1 head cabbage cut into wedges
½ cup water
¼ cup flour

In a large heavy pan, brown meat in shortening and drain off fat. Add onion soup, horseradish and garlic salt, and simmer for 2 hours covered. Add carrots and simmer another 30 minutes stirring occasionally. Then add potatoes and cabbage and cook another 30 minutes or until tender. Remove meat and vegetables and put on serving dish. Blend water into flour and stir into sauce in skillet. Cook while stirring until thickened. Pour over meat and potatoes.

POTATO HASH

Boil potatoes, remove jackets and put through meat grinder with any kind of beef (or corned beef). Add chopped onions and fry in vegetable oil. Sprinkle with salt and pepper to taste.

POTATO-POLISH SAUSAGE CASSEROLE

¼ cup butter or margarine
1 cup chopped onion
3 T. flour
2 cups milk
½ t. salt

¼ t. pepper
2 cups shredded cheese (Swiss, Cheddar, American)
2 pounds potatoes, peeled, cooked and sliced
1 pound Polish Sausage (hot dogs), sliced

Melt butter or margarine in medium saucepan. Add onion and saute' until tender. Blend in flour. Add milk and stir until mixture boils and thickens. Add salt and pepper. Remove from heat and stir in 1½ cups cheese.

Alternate layers of 1/2 potatoes and sausage. Pour on half the sauce, then layer remaining potatoes and sausage and pour on remaining sauce. Sprinkle with remaining cheese. Preheat oven to 350 degrees. Bake 45-60 minutes uncovered. Makes 8 servings. (Can be made up to 24 hours before cooking.)

POTATOES AND BEEF

1 package instant scalloped potatoes
1 pound ground beef
1 can tomatoes
1 cup chopped celery

1 medium onion
1 t. salt
½ t. pepper
1 cup water

Place potato slices into baking dish. Brown ground beef and drain. Stir in tomatoes, celery, onion, salt, pepper, and water and package of sauce mix. Simmer a few minutes and pour over potatoes. Bake, covered, at 350 degrees for 45 minutes.

POTATO PIZZA

1 package instant scalloped potatoes
1 16 oz. can tomatoes
1 cup water
¼ t. oregano

½ pound ground beef, browned or
½ pound ground pork sausage, browned or
4 oz. sliced pepperoni
4 oz. shredded mozzarella cheese

Place potato slices into ungreased baking dish. Sprinkle packet of seasoned sauce mix (comes with packaged scalloped potatoes) over potatoes. Bring to a boil tomatoes, water, and oregano. Add ground beef, ground pork or pepperoni to potatoes. Pour tomato mixture over this and sprinkle with cheese. Bake uncovered for 30 minutes at 375 degrees.

SKILLET POTATOES AND HAM

2 T. butter
5-6 medium potatoes
1 medium onion
1½ cup milk
1 t. salt

¼ t. pepper
1 T. catsup
½ t. Worcestershire sauce
1 cup diced cheese
2 cup diced, cooked ham

Melt butter in skillet. Add thinly sliced potatoes and chopped onion. Stir well. Add milk and seasonings. Put cheese and ham over top and cover. Simmer on low for about 45 minutes or until tender.

POTATO-TACO PIE

¼ cup butter
½ cup milk
1 1¼ oz. package taco seasoning mix
2 cups instant mashed potato flakes
1 pound ground beef
1 medium onion, chopped

1 can brown beans
½ cup barbecue sauce
¼ cup water
1 cup shredded cheese
1 cup shredded lettuce
1 cup chopped tomato

Melt butter in saucepan. Add milk and 2 T. of the dry taco seasoning mix. Remove from heat and stir in potato flakes. Press this mixture into bottom of ungreased pie plate. Brown ground beef and onion in a skillet and drain off fat. Stir in beans, barbecue sauce, water, and remaining taco mix. Cook until bubbly while stirring. Put into pie pan and bake for 30-40 minutes at 325 degrees. Top with cheese, lettuce and tomato.

HAM AND POTATO LOAF

4 cups chopped cooked ham
¾ cup mayonnaise
½ cup diced celery
½ cup diced sweet pickle

3 T. pickle juice
1 t. salt
2 pounds potatoes cooked, peeled and cubed

Mix ham and 1/2 cup mayonnaise and press in bottom of loaf pan lined with paper. Mix remaining ingredients with 1/4 cup mayonnaise. Press over ham layer. Cover and chill for about 4-5 hours.

BRATWURST AND POTATOES

8 medium potatoes
8 slices bacon
½ cup chopped onion
½ cup chopped celery
2 T. flour

2 T. sugar
2 t. salt
½ cup water
2 packages bratwurst
2 T. shortening

Peel potatoes, slice and boil until tender. Drain and cool. Fry bacon until crisp. Saute' onion and celery in bacon drippings. Blend in flour, sugar, and salt. Add water. Cook while stirring until mixture has thickened.

Crumble bacon. Stir bacon crumbs and potato slices into hot mixture. Brown bratwurst in shortening and serve with potatoes.

CHICKEN GRATIN POTATOES

2-3 T. soft butter
2 cups chopped onion
12 medium potatoes, peeled and sliced

Dash of salt and pepper
3 cups of grated Swiss cheese
2 cups chicken stock

Saute' onions in butter. Put one layer of potatoes in buttered baking dish and season with salt and pepper. On top of this, spread layer of onion and cheese. Continue with two more layers of potato, onion and cheese (using only 2 cups of cheese.) Dot with butter and pour in enough chicken stock to fill one-half the dish.

Bake for 35 minutes at 400 degrees.

Cut baking hens into pieces and brown. Place chicken pieces over the potatoes and spread remaining 1 cup cheese over them. Baste with juices cooked in potatoes and any remaining chicken stock not already used. Bake for 30 minutes more until all is tender.

HAM HOCKS AND POTATOES

3-4 pounds fresh ham hocks
2 t. salt
3 medium onions, sliced

3 celery stalks, chopped
1 bay leaf
4-6 medium potatoes, peeled and quartered

Wash ham hocks thoroughly in cold water. Put first 5 ingredients in large kettle. Cover and bring to a boil. Simmer for 2 hours. Add potatoes and simmer for 30-40 minutes longer (or until ham and potatoes are tender.

RABBIT-POTATOES STEW

¼ cup olive oil
2 T. brandy
2 domestic rabbits, cut up
1 large chopped onion
2 cloves garlic, minced
2 T. olive oil

1 can tomatoes, cut up
1 t. salt
5 medium potatoes
3 medium carrots
2 stalks celery

In a large bowl combine olive oil and brandy and pour over rabbit. Cover, refrigerate and marinade for 2 to 3 hours.

In a saucepan saute' onions in the olive oil. Add undrained tomatoes and simmer for 5-6 minutes. Add rabbit pieces, marinade, and salt, and simmer for 30 minutes. Add potatoes, carrots and celery. Cover and simmer for 30 minutes longer.

Hot & Cold Potato Salads

CHICKEN-POTATO SALAD

2 cups cooked cubed chicken
1 cup cooked cubed potatoes
1 cup chopped raw apple
1 cup pineapple chunks, drained
1 cup raisins
½ cup chopped green olives

½ cup chopped sweet pickles
½ cup chopped celery
½ cup toasted almonds
2 hard boiled eggs, diced
1 cup mayonnaise
Dash of salt and pepper

Combine all ingredients, toss lightly. Cover and chill before serving. Crush potato chips over salad before serving if desired. Serve on lettuce leaves.

SHOESTRING POTATO-MEAT SALAD

1 can shoestring potatoes
2 cups cooked chicken or tuna, cubed
1 cup chopped celery
1 small onion, minced
1 large apple, chopped

1 cup shredded carrots
½ cup mayonnaise
½ cup cream
1 T. dry mustard
1 T. sugar

Combine all ingredients and toss gently. Cover and refrigerate until flavors are blended.

POTATO SALAD WITH CHICKEN AND HAM

2 cups cubed, cooked chicken
2 cups cubed, cooked ham
2 cups cubed, cooked potatoes
1 medium onion, chopped
1 cup chopped celery

2 boiled eggs, diced
1 cup mayonnaise
1 T. sugar
1 t. salt

Chill first 3 ingredients. When chilled, add remaining ingredients and toss gently. Serve cold.

GERMAN POTATO SALAD

8 slices bacon, crumbled
5-6 medium potatoes
1 medium onion, chopped
Salt and pepper
1 t. dry mustard

½ cup sugar
¼ cup water
¼ cup vinegar
1 egg, beaten

Fry bacon crisp and save drippings. Cook potatoes in boiling water until tender, remove skins and slice. Combine potatoes, onion and bacon crumbs. Add salt, pepper, dry mustard, sugar, water, vinegar and egg to bacon grease. Cook until egg thickens. Pour this over potato mixture and bake in oven at 350 degrees for 15 minutes. Garnish with bacon crumbs if desired.

VEGETABLE SALAD

1 cup cooked beans
2 cups cooked, cubed potatoes
2 tomatoes, cubed
1 cup ham, chicken, or beef, cubed
3 boiled eggs, chopped
½ cup chopped sweet pickles
1 head of lettuce, torn apart

Dressing:
¾ cup salad oil
¼ cup vinegar
¼ t. dry mustard
Dash of pepper
1 T. sugar

Toss together first 7 ingredients and chill. When ready to serve, shake the ingredients for the dressing and add to the salad.

CHICKEN - POTATO SALAD - II

1 cup chopped celery
1 medium onion, diced
2 apples, unpeeled and cubed
1 cup grated carrots
1 ½ cup cooked chicken, cubed

1 cup mayonnaise
1 T. dry mustard
1 T. sugar
1 t. salt
1 can shoestring potatoes

Combine first 5 ingredients and chill. Mix together mayonnaise, mustard, sugar and salt, and stir into chilled ingredients. When ready to serve, stir shoestring potatoes into salad.

HAM - POTATO SALAD

2 cups cooked cubed potatoes
1 cup cooked cubed ham
1 cup diced celery
¼ cup diced sweet pickles
2 hard-boiled eggs, diced
1 pimiento, chopped
½ cup chopped olives

1 medium green pepper, minced
½ cup mayonnaise
½ cup sour cream
1 t. dry mustard
1 t. salt
1 T. sugar
Dash of pepper

Combine first 8 ingredients and chill. Mix together last 6 ingredients and stir into salad. Serve on lettuce if desired.

MEAT - POTATO SALAD

1 head of lettuce, torn into pieces
2-3 cubed potatoes
1 chopped green pepper
1 chopped cucumber
1 cup cubed ham or luncheon meat
2 hard-boiled eggs, chopped

½ cup salad dressing
¼ cup cream
1 T. vinegar
Dash of salt and pepper
¼ t. dry mustard

Combine first 6 ingredients and toss gently. Shake together salad dressing, cream, vinegar, salt, pepper and mustard and pour over salad. Toss again and chill.

CHEESE - POTATO SALAD

2 pounds cooked, cubed potatoes
½ pound cubed Swiss cheese
3 cups cooked green peas
2 hard boiled eggs, chopped
1 cup chopped pimiento
1 small onion, minced

Dressing:
1 cup mayonnaise
¼ cup French dressing
1 T. dry mustard
2 T. lemon juice
1 T. Worcestershire sauce
½ t. salt
Dash of paprika
Dash of pepper

Mix together first 6 ingredients. Shake together in a jar the ingredients for the dressing. Fold dressing into potato mixture and chill

BEAN-POTATO SALAD

2 cups cooked chopped meat
1 cup cooked chopped potatoes
½ cup cooked diced carrot
1 cup cooked green beans
1 cup French dressing

½ cup chopped sweet pickles
2 hard boiled eggs, chopped
1 cup mayonnaise
Dash of salt and pepper

Combine all ingredients. Toss gently. Let chill for at least 1 hour and serve on lettuce leaf.

POTATO-HOT DOG SALAD

1 pound hot dogs, boiled
6 medium potatoes, cooked
2 hard boiled eggs, chopped
½ cup chopped sweet pickles
½ cup chopped celery

½ cup chopped pimiento
1 cup mayonnaise
1 t. dry mustard
1 t. salt
Dash of pepper

Chop hot dogs and potatoes into small pieces and chill for several hours. Add the remaining ingredients and toss lightly to blend. Serve cold.

CREAMY POTATO SALAD

10 medium potatoes
3 boiled eggs
¾ cup mayonnaise
1 t. dry mustard
¾ cup sour cream
1 t. salt

¼ t. pepper
12 slices bacon
¼ cup chopped onion
½ cup chopped celery
¼ cup Italian salad dressing

Cook potatoes until tender. Drain and cool. Peel potatoes and cut into cubes. Chop eggs, stir in mayonnaise, mustard, sour cream, salt and pepper and add to potatoes. Cook bacon until crisp and crumble. Add to potatoes the bacon crumbs, onion, celery and Italian dressing. Toss gently. Chill.

MEAT - POTATO SALAD - II

2 cups cooked choped ham, beef, pork
2 hard boiled eggs, chopped
1 cup cooked chopped potatoes
½ cup finely chopped sweet pickle
½ cup finely chopped celery

½ cup chopped pecans
1 large red apple, pared and diced
1 cup mayonnaise
1 t. sugar
1 t. salt

Combine all ingredients. Toss gently and chill.

SOUR CREAM-POTATO SALAD

1 cup chopped luncheon meat
3 cups chopped cooked potatoes
2 hard boiled eggs
1 t. salt
¼ t. pepper
¼ cup diced sweet pickles

¼ cup diced green pepper
1 small onion, minced
1 T. vinegar
1 T. dry mustard
½ cup mayonnaise
½ cup sour cream

Combine first 8 ingredients and toss gently. Blend together vinegar, mustard, mayonnaise and sour cream. Fold into potato mixture. Chill for several hours until flavors are well blended.

CORNED BEEF AND POTATO SALAD

4 medium potatoes, cooked and cubed
1 12 oz. can corned beef, shredded
2 T. diced onion
2 T. chopped sweet pickles

2 hard boiled eggs, chopped
1 cup chopped celery
2 T. chopped green pepper
1 cup mayonnaise

Combine all ingredients. Mix together lightly. Cover and chill for several hours.

HOT POTATO SALAD

1 pound frozen french fried potatoes
1 green pepper, chopped
1 medium onion, diced
1 cup cubed meat

4 T. French dressing
1 cup shredded cheese
Dash of salt and pepper

Brown french fries in shortening and drain. Add green pepper, onion, meat and French dressing. Simmer until meat is lightly browned. Sprinkle with salt and pepper, and top with shredded cheese. Serve warm.

ITALIAN POTATO SALAD

4 medium potatoes cooked
1 medium onion, sliced
½ chopped parsley

Italian dressing to taste
1 t. celery seed
6 chopped radishes

Combine chopped potatoes, sliced onion rings, chopped parsley, Italian dressing, celery seed and radishes. Mix together well and chill. Serve cold.

SAUSAGE-POTATO SALAD

3-4 large new potatoes
4-5 hot sausages
¼ cup cooking wine
1 cup plain yogurt
1 small onion, minced
1 T. vinegar

½ t. salt
¼ t. pepper
4 boiled eggs, sliced
2 tomatoes, sliced
Lettuce

Cook potatoes in boiling salted water until tender. Cool and peel. Chop into cubes. Marinate sausages in wine for about 1 hour. Then simmer in wine for 10 minutes while covered. Uncover pan and let sausage brown. Drain and cool sausages. Cut into slices.

Combine yogurt, onion, vinegar, salt and pepper. Pour this over the potatoes and toss lightly. Arrange the potato salad and sausage on lettuce leaves and garnish with slices of eggs and tomatoes.

HOT POTATO SALAD - II

6 medium potatoes
1 carton sour cream
1 can cream of celery soup
1 cup shredded cheddar cheese

4 boiled eggs, chopped
1 chopped onion
1 T. chopped parsley

Cook potatoes until tender. Cool. Peel and cut potatoes into cubes. Combine sour cream, soup, cheese, eggs, onion and parsley. Add this to potatoes and stir well. Spread in baking dish and bake at 350 degrees for 30 minutes. Serve warm.

BEAN POTATO SALAD

1 pound new potatoes, peeled and cubed
1 pound fresh green beans
8 slices bacon
½ cup chopped onion
¼ cup mayonnaise

1 T. vinegar
1 t. salt
½ t. garlic salt
¼ t. white pepper

Cook potatoes and green beans in salted water, covered, until tender. Drain water off.

Fry bacon, remove from skillet and drain. Saute' onion in bacon grease and stir onions into potatoes-beans. Combine mayonnaise, vinegar, salts and pepper and pour over vegetables, stirring well. Add bacon crumbs and toss gently. Serve while warm.

DILL POTATO SALAD

1 T. butter
1 T. flour
1 cup milk
1 t. salt
¼ t. dried dillweed

¼ t. pepper
½ cup mayonnaise
1 medium onion, minced
4 cups diced cooked potatoes

Melt butter over low heat. Blend in flour and gradually add milk, stirring constantly, until thick and bubbly. Stir in salt, dillweed, pepper and mayonnaise, stirring well. Stir in onion and potatoes. Serve warm.

DILL-POTATO SALAD - II

1 cup sour cream
1 cup mayonnaise
½ cup dill pickles, chopped

1 T. salt
½ t. pepper
8-10 cooked potatoes, peeled, cubed and chilled

Mix together first 5 ingredients. Pour over potatoes and toss lightly. Chill and serve.

GREEN PEPPER POTATO SALAD

6 medium potatoes
4 slices bacon
1/3 cup vinegar
½ cup sugar
½ t. salt

¼ t. pepper
½ cup chopped celery
1 small chopped onion
2 T. pimiento, chopped
3 or 4 large green peppers

Cook potatoes until tender in boiling salted water. Cool and peel potatoes. Cube potatoes and set aside.

Fry bacon until crisp and crumble. Save 2 tablespoons drippings. Add to bacon grease the vinegar, sugar, salt and pepper and cook over medium heat for about 3 minutes. Combine potatoes, bacon crumbs, celery, onion and pimiento. Add to this the cooked dressing, stirring completely.

Cut green peppers in half, remove inside of peppers and cook in boiling salted water about 3 minutes. Remove from water and drain. Place peppers on plates and fill them with warm potato mixtures. Serve warm.

29

HOT POTATO SALAD

8 medium potatoes
1 t. salt
½ t. celery seeds
⅛ t. pepper
6 slices bacon

1 medium chopped onion
½ cup vinegar
2 T. sugar
1 beaten egg
1 T. minced parsley

Cook potatoes until tender in boiling salted water. Cool slightly. Peel and slice potatoes. Add salt, celery seeds and pepper.

Fry bacon until crisp and drain. Saute' onion in bacon drippings. Add onions to potatoes. Add vinegar, sugar and egg to remaining drippings and simmer for 2 minutes. Add this to potato mixture. Add bacon and parsley to potatoes and toss. Serve warm.

SOUR CREAM POTATO SALAD

8-10 med. potatoes, cooked, peeled and sliced
1 cup chopped green onion
1½ cups mayonnaise
1 carton sour cream (8 oz.)

1 t. celery seed
1 t. horseradish
1 cup minced parsley

Mix mayonnaise, sour cream, horseradish and celery seeds and set aside. Place half of potatoes in a dish, sprinkle with 1/3 cup parsley and 1/4 cup onion. Then add half of mayonnaise mixture. Repeat again the layers. Garnish the top with parsley. Cover and chill.

POTATO SALAD

12 med. potatoes, cooked, peeled and diced
1 medium onion, chopped
1 medium green pepper, chopped
2-3 stalks celery, sliced thin
1 T. parsley, minced
1 medium carrot, shredded

4-6 large olives, sliced
6 boiled eggs, chopped
1 bottle (12 oz.) commercial slaw dressing
1/3 cup commercial sour cream
2 T. lemon juice or vinegar

Cook potatoes until tender in boiling water in which 1 T. salt and 1 T. lemon juice have been added. Peel, dice, and chill potatoes. Combine potatoes and next 7 ingredients in a large bowl. Combine slaw dressing, sour cream, and 2 T. lemon juice and stir well. Add this dressing to potato salad and stir gently. Serve cold.

POTATO SALAD-SCALLOPED

1 box packaged scalloped potatoes
3 cups water
3 T. salad oil
½ cup water
¼ cup vinegar

½ cup mayonnaise
¼ t. mustard
½ cup chopped celery
½ cup minced onion
4 boiled eggs, chopped

Cook potatoes in 3 cups water until tender. Drain, cover and chill. Blend sauce mix (in box), oil, water, and vinegar, and heat to boiling, stirring constantly. Remove from heat. Cover and chill. Blend mayonnaise, mustard, celery, onion and eggs and stir into chilled sauce. Fold this into chilled potatoes and serve.

POTATO-SARDINE SALAD

6 medium potatoes
2 chopped celery stalks
1 can drained sardines
½ cup sour cream
¼ cup mayonnaise

1 T. lemon juice
½ t. dry mustard
½ t. salt
¼ t. pepper
2 T. chopped parsley

Cook potatoes, peel and cube. Add the celery. Mash sardines in a bowl. Add next 6 ingredients and mix well. Add the sardine mixture to the potatoes and celery and toss together. Sprinkle with parsley. Serve cold.

HOT GERMAN POTATO SALAD

4 medium potatoes
1 small minced onion
2 T. flour
1 T. sugar
1 t. salt

½ t. pepper
1 t. celery seeds
4 slices bacon
¼ cup vinegar
1 T. chopped parsley

Cook potatoes until tender. Cool potatoes. Peel, cube and place in a baking dish. Combine next 6 ingredients and spread over potatoes. Fry bacon until crisp. Save bacon drippings. Crumble bacon. Stir vinegar into 2 tablespoons drippings and pour over potato mixture. Sprinkle bacon crumbs over potatoes. Bake at 350 degrees for 30 minutes. Serve warm. Garnish with parsley.

POTATO AND CORNED BEEF-SALAD

4 cups cooked potatoes, peeled and cubed
1 can corned beef, cubed
½ cup chopped celery
½ cup chopped onion
¼ cup salad oil

2 T. vinegar
1 t. salt
¼ t. pepper
½ cup sour cream
2 T. horseradish

Toss together potatoes, meat, celery and onion. Shake together oil, vinegar, salt and pepper in a jar. Pour this over potato mixture and toss. Chill for 2-4 hours, covered. Mix sour cream and horseradish and pour over potato mixture when ready to serve.

APPLE-POTATO SALAD

5 cups cooked, cubed potatoes
1 cup chopped celery
1 medium green pepper, diced
2 cups red apples, cubed
1 small onion, diced

1 cup mayonnaise
1 T. vinegar
2 T. sugar
1 t. salt

Combine first 5 ingredients. Mix together mayonnaise, vinegar, sugar and salt and stir into potato mixture. Toss gently. Serve cold.

33

PARMESAN POTATO SALAD

6 slices bacon
4 cups sliced cooked potatoes
½ cup sliced onion

½ cup Italian dressing
½ cup Parmesan cheese
Dash of salt and pepper

Fry bacon until crisp. Crumble bacon. Combine bacon, potatoes, onion and dressing in a pan and cook over low heat until completely heated. Stir in cheese. Sprinkle with salt and pepper. Serve while still warm.

POTATO SALAD WITH COTTAGE CHEESE

3 cups cooked potatoes (cubed)
½ cup chopped celery
1 T. chopped green pepper
2 T. minced onion
1 T. chopped pimientos

2 T. chopped sweet pickle
1 T. lemon juice
1 t. salt
1 cup mayonnaise
1 cup cottage cheese

Combine all ingredients, mixing well. Refrigerate until chilled.

SKEWERED POTATOES

4 medium potatoes, baked,
   unpeeled, quartered
4 tomatoes, quartered

1-2 zucchinis, sliced
4 green peppers, quartered
Italian dressing

Marinate cooked potato quarters, tomato wedges, zucchini slices and green pepper quarters in Italian dressing. Spear on skewers and serve.

POTATO-SPINACH SALAD

4-6 medium new potatoes, unpeeled
Fresh mushrooms halved
Onions sliced

Fresh spinach
½ package fried bacon, crumbled
1 cup Italian dressing

Cook potatoes in boiling salted water until tender. Drain, cool and slice. Marinate potato slices, mushroom halves and sliced onion rings in Italian dressing for 1-2 hours. Then toss with spinach and crumbled bacon. Serve cold.

POTATO SALAD - II

4 cups cooked, peeled, cubed potatoes
4 boiled eggs, chopped
1 large onion, chopped
½ cup chopped celery
1 cup mayonnaise

3 T. mustard
1 small can pimientos, chopped
2 large cucumbers, chopped
1 cup ripe olives
Season with salt and pepper

Toss gently the first 9 ingredients. Season to taste with salt and pepper. Chill for several hours.

GARDEN POTATO SALAD

5-6 cups cooked, cubed, chilled potatoes
½ cup chopped green onion
1 cup chopped zucchini
1 cup chopped celery
1 large tomato, chopped

1 cucumber, diced
½ cup vinegar
½ cup salad oil
1 t. salt
Dash garlic salt

Combine all ingredients and toss gently to mix. Serve chilled.

POTATO SALAD WITH SOUR CREAM

2 boiled eggs, chopped
1 cup mayonnaise
½ cup sour cream
1 t. mustard
½ t. horseradish

6 slices bacon, fried crisp & crumble
½ cup minced green onion
8-10 medium cooked, cubed, chilled potatoes
½ cup Italian salad dressing
Dash of salt & pepper

Mix together all the above ingredients and toss lightly until blended. Garnish with tomato wedges and/or parsley.

SALAMI-POTATO SALAD

3 cups cooked potatoes, cubed
2 cups cubed salami
1 cup peas, canned or cooked
½ cup pimiento
1 cup diced celery
½ cup chopped sweet pickles

1 small onion, minced
2 hard boiled eggs, chopped
1 cup mayonnaise
1 T. vinegar
1 t. dry mustard
Dash of salt and pepper and chopped parsley

Combine all ingredients and toss lightly. Chill for several hours and garnish with parsley if desired.

Soup & Chowders

POTATO SEAFOOD CHOWDER

1 medium potato, peeled and diced
1 medium onion, diced
1 pint oysters
¼ cup melted butter
2 T. flour

Dash of salt and pepper
1 can clams minced
2 cans shrimp, chopped
1 quart scalded milk

Cook potato and onion in boiling salted water until tender. Drain water off.

Cook oysters in butter for several minutes on low. Combine flour, salt, pepper, and add to oysters. Add potatoes, onion, clams, shrimp and scalded milk. Blend until smooth. Heat and serve.

NEW ENGLAND CLAM CHOWDER

4 cups diced, peeled potatoes
4 oz. salt pork, minced
1 pint fresh shucked clams or/
2-7½ oz. cans clams
2 cups water

1 cup cream
3 T. flour
2 t. salt
1 medium onion, diced
2 cups milk

Cook salt pork until crisp. Remove any lean portion of pork and save. Add potatoes, water, onion and cook, uncovered, until potatoes are tender. Add diced clams, 1¾ cups milk, and the cream.

Blend together the remaining 1/4 cup milk and flour and stir into chowder. Heat to boiling. Add salt, pepper and salt pork. Stir occasionally.

POTATO POTAGE

2 cups diced potatoes
1 cup sliced onion
2 quarts water
1 T. salt

2 T. parsley
1 cup whipping cream
1 can undiluted chicken broth

Combine potatoes, onions, water and salt in a saucepan and bring to a boil. Reduce heat and simmer for one hour. Then mash vegetables in liquid and cool. Stir in parsley, whipping cream and chicken broth. Chill. Serve cold.

POTATO CHOWDER

1/4 cup diced salt pork
1 cup sliced celery
1 medium chopped onion
2 cans cream of potato soup

2 soup cans milk
1 pound filet of white fish, cut up
1 cup sliced cooked carrots
Dash of salt and pepper

Brown salt pork in a saucepan. Remove. Saute' onions and celery in drippings until tender. Add salt pork and remaining ingredients. Bring to a boil and reduce heat to a simmer. Cook for 10-15 minutes on low, stirring often.

POTATO-TOMATO SOUP

2 T. bacon grease
2 medium potatoes, peeled and cubed
2 cups milk

1 cup canned tomatoes
Flour
Milk

Boil potatoes in boiling salted water with 2 T. bacon grease. When potatoes are tender, pour off all but 1/2 cup of water. Add milk, tomatoes. Heat to boiling and thicken with a sauce made from milk and flour. Serve hot.

CREAM OF POTATO SOUP

Melt 2 T. butter or margarine
Blend in: 2 T. flour — ¼ t. salt
Add 1 cup milk — cook quickly, stirring constantly until mixture thickens and bubbles. This makes 1 cup sauce.
Add 2 cups diced, cooked potatoes and 1 tablespoon chopped canned pimientos to 3 cups sauce above. Stir well. Serve hot.

POTATO SOUP

3 cups peeled, diced potatoes
1 cup boiling water
1 t. salt

1 small onion
½ t. white pepper
2 cups sour cream

Put the first 5 ingredients in a medium size heavy saucepan and cook for 15 minutes. Add sour cream and simmer until tender.

POTATO SOUP

3-4 medium potatoes
2 cups milk
½ t. salt
Dash of pepper

1 T. melted butter
4 T. flour
1 beaten egg

Boil potatoes until tender, peel and mash. Scald 2 cups milk. Blend potatoes, salt and pepper into scalded milk. Combine butter, flour and beaten egg and add to potatoes. Cook, covered about 5-10 minutes over low heat.

CREAM OF POTATO SOUP — II

3-4 cups diced potatoes
1 cup chopped celery
1 medium onion, chopped
2 T. butter

½ t. salt
¼ t. pepper
2 cups half-and-half
2 T. flour

Combine first 6 ingredients in saucepan and cook in water until tender. Drain water. Combine half-and-half and flour and stir until flour is dissolved. Gradually add to tender vegetables and simmer gently until thick and bubbly.

Hot Potatoes

CHEESED SPUDS

Scrub baking potatoes. Cut into strips. Place strips on foil and sprinkle with onion salt, celery salt, parmesan cheese and pepper. Then dot with butter. Seal edges of foil together and cook on grill over coals, turning several times, about 30-45 minutes.

HOT POTATOES

4 medium baking potatoes	½ pound Cheddar cheese
1 medium onion, chopped	6 slices bacon, fried crisp
1 stick butter or margarine, sliced	Salt and pepper

Bake potatoes in oven until done. Cool potatoes, peel and slice. Wrap potato slices, onions, butter, salt and pepper in aluminum foil. Cook in oven or on a grill for one hour. Open foil and add cubed cheese and crumbled bacon pieces. Close foil and cook 20 minutes more.

VOLCANO POTATOES

Cook and mash 4-6 potatoes. Season with salt and pepper. Whip with 3/4 cup of hot milk. Pile into greased 8″ round baking dish, mounding into volcano shape. Make crater in center. Fold 1/2 cup shredded sharp processed cheese into 1/2 cup whipping cream, whipped. Pour into crater. Bake at 350 degrees about 20 minutes or until lightly browned.

SCALLOPED POTATOES WITH PIMIENTO

5 cups cooked sliced potatoes
4 T. Ch. pimiento
1 medium green pepper, chopped
3 T. butter or margarine
4 T. all purpose flour

1½ cups milk
½ t. salt
¼ t. pepper
½ cup shredded Cheddar cheese

Combine potatoes, pimiento and green pepper. Spoon into a greased 2 qt. casserole.

Melt butter in saucepan. Add flour and milk gradually, stirring constantly, until thick and bubbly. Stir in salt and pepper. Remove from heat, add cheese and stir until melted.

Pour cheese over potato mixture. Bake at 350 degrees for 45-55 minutes. Serves 8.

SCALLOPED POTATOES

8-10 large potatoes, peeled and sliced
1 onion, diced
½ stick butter
½ cup flour

½ t. dry mustard
2 cups milk
1 pound (4 cups) shredded Cheddar Cheese
¼ cup bread crumbs

Cook potatoes and onion in salted water until tender. Melt butter in a large saucepan, add flour and mustard, stirring until smooth. Add milk gradually, stirring all the time, and cook until thick and bubbly. Add chesse and stir until cheese melts.

DOUBLE POTATO BAKE

4 servings packaged instant hash browns
1 10½ oz. can condensed cream of potato soup
1 soup can milk
1 T. instant minced onion
1 T. snipped parsley
1/3 cup shredded Parmesan cheese
Salt and pepper

Prepare potatoes according to directions on box. Combine soup, milk, onion, parsley, and a dash of salt and pepper. Heat soup and add to potatoes. Put into baking dish and sprinkle with cheese. Heat at 325 degrees for 30 minutes.

GRILLED LEMON POTATOES

4 large potatoes, peeled and sliced
¼ cup melted butter
¼ cup lemon juice
1 t. salt
¼ t. nutmeg
¼ t. pepper
1 green onion, chopped

Cook potatoes until tender in boiling, salted water. Refrigerate potatoes until chilled. Combine remaining ingredients and toss gently. Spread onto large piece of double-thick aluminum foil and wrap tightly.

Place on grill and cook 15 minutes. Turn and cook 15 minutes longer.

HOT DEVILED POTATOES

Packaged instant mashed potatoes
½ cup sour cream
2 t. prepared mustard

½ t. salt
½ t. sugar
2 T. chopped green onion

Prepare potatoes according to directions on package. Heat sour cream, add mustard, 1/2 t. salt and sugar, stir. Mix into hot potatoes with onion. Put in a 1-quart casserole. Bake at 350 degrees for 10 minutes. Serves 4.

POTATO CROQUETTES

2 cups of mashed potatoes
2 T. butter
1 egg
Pepper

Salt
1 small chopped onion
1 T. chopped parsley
Dash of cayenne

Mix the above ingredients and shape into balls. Dip balls in beaten egg and roll in cracker crumbs. Fry in deep fat.

GOOD OL' MASHED POTATOES

2 pounds potatoes
4 cups water

½ cup milk
¼ cup melted butter or margarine

Peel potatoes and cut up. Cook in boiling, salted water until tender — about 20 minutes. Pour water off. Mash by hand or with electric mixer until no lumps remain. Melt butter, and pour butter along with milk into hot potatoes. Add salt and pepper to desired taste. Serve hot.

GRILLED POTATOES

4 medium potatoes
Salt and pepper

½ cup Italian salad dressing

Cook potatoes until tender. While still hot, cut potatoes into 1/2 inch slices. Place in shallow dish and pour salad dressing over hot slices. Let stand 45 minutes, turning once.

Place on grill. Cook 8-10 minutes on each side until golden brown. Sprinkle with salt and pepper.

POTATOES AND PEAS

¼ cup butter
¼ cup flour
1 t. salt
¼ t. pepper
2 cups milk

1 cup shredded Cheddar cheese
1 pkg. frozen green peas
3 cups sliced, cooked potatoes
1 2 oz. jar chopped pimiento

Melt butter in a saucepan. Stir in flour, salt and pepper until smooth. Stir in milk and cook until smooth and thick.

Add cheese and stir until melted. Remove from heat.

Cook peas in boiling salted water until slightly tender. Drain and combine with potatoes and pimiento in a greased casserole dish. Pour cheese sauce over top and sprinkle with bread crumbs. Bake at 350 degrees for 30-40 minutes.

GRILLED ONIONS POTATOES

½ cup butter, softened

4 medium baking potatoes

1 envelope onion soup mix

Scrub potatoes and dry off. Cut potatoes into 1/2" slices. Combine butter and soup mix. Put potatoes back together, wrap in Reynold's wrap, and pour soup mixture over the potatoes, making sure that each slice of the potato is coated.

Cook potatoes on the grill over medium heat about 1 hour turning several times.

BARBECUED POTATOES

3 T. butter

3 T. flour

1 t. salt

2 cups milk

1 T. chopped parsley

2 T. chopped pimientos

1 t. hot sauce

4-5 cups cooked, diced potatoes

1 cup soft bread crumbs

1 T. melted butter

1 cup shredded cheddar cheese

Melt butter in saucepan. Add flour and salt, stirring until smooth. Slowly add the milk, stirring constantly, cooking all the time, until the mixture thickens. Stir in parsley, pimientos, hot sauce and potatoes, and pour into a greased baking dish. Combine bread crumbs, melted butter, cheese and sprinkle over potato mixture. Bake at 350 degrees for 25-30 minutes.

CELERY AND CHEESE POTATOES

5-6 medium potatoes
1 small onion, minced
1 can cream of celery soup

½ soup can milk
1 cup grated cheddar cheese
Dash of salt and pepper

Peel potatoes, slice and cook in boiling salted water until tender. Mix together onions, soup, milk, cheese, salt and pepper, and heat until cheese is melted. Pour mixture over layered sliced potatoes. Bake at 350 degrees for 30 minutes.

MUSTARD POTATOES

4 medium potatoes
1 small onion, diced
4 T. butter
2 T. flour
1 chicken bouillon cube

1 t. salt
½ t. pepper
1½ T. mustard
1 T. Parmesan cheese
Bread crumbs

Peel potatoes and slice. Cook in boiling water until tender. Drain water off and pour potatoes into greased casserole dish. Saute' onion in butter and stir in flour until smooth. Dissolve bouillon cube in 3/4 cup boiling water. Stir this into flour and butter mixture. Cook while stirring until sauce thickens and bubbles. Stir in salt, pepper and mustard. Simmer for 5-6 minutes and pour over potatoes. Combine bread crumbs and parmesan cheese and sprinkle over casserole. Bake at 350 degrees for 15 minutes.

STUFFED POTATOES

6 baking potatoes
1 package cream cheese (8 oz.)
1 small can deviled ham (4 oz.)

1 small onion, diced
3 T. mayonnaise
1 T. parmesan cheese, grated

Bake potatoes until completely done. Combine cream cheese, ham, onion, and mayonnaise and set aside. After potatoes have cooled, cut in half, lengthwise, and scoop out pulp. Whip together potatoes and cream cheese mixture until smooth. Stuff potato shells with potato-cheese mixture. Sprinkle with parmesan cheese. Heat in oven at 350 degrees until hot.

MUSHROOM POTATOES

6 large potatoes
½ cup melted butter
¼ cup half and half
1 medium onion
Salt and pepper

4 T. butter
1 8 oz. can sliced mushrooms
¼ cup flour
¼ cup milk

Bake potatoes until completely done. Cut potatoes in half and scoop out inside. Mash pulp of potato, add butter, half and half, salt and pepper. Chop onions and saute' in butter. Add mushrooms and flour. Stir. Add milk and cook until thick. Add to potatoes. Put mixture back into potato shell. Place in 350 degree oven and brown for 15 minutes.

SESAME POTATOES

6 medium potatoes
1 cup sesame seeds

½ cup melted butter
Dash garlic salt and pepper

Scrub potatoes well. Cut potatoes into thin strips (lengthwise). Dip potatoes in butter. Coat both sides with sesame seeds. Place on a greased baking sheet and sprinkle with salt and pepper. Bake at 375 degrees for 35-40 minutes or until done.

SHRIMP POTATOES

4 large baking potatoes
½ stick butter
1 can cream of shrimp soup

½ t. salt
1/8 t. pepper
Shredded cheddar cheese

Bake potatoes until tender. Cool potatoes and cut lengthwise. Scoop out pulp and mash with butter, soup, salt and pepper. Stuff potatoes and sprinkle with cheese. Put back into oven and bake until cheese melts.

CHEESE POTATOES

4-5 medium potatoes
6 slices bacon
1 medium onion

½ pound Cheddar cheese, cubed
1 stick butter or margarine

Peel potatoes, cook in water until tender, cool and cube. Place on foil paper and sprinkle with salt and pepper. Crumble bacon over. Add onion and cubed cheese. Slice butter over. Mix together and seal paper. Cook in oven or over coals until cheese melts.

HASH BROWN POTATO CASSEROLE

1 package frozen hash brown
   potatoes, thawed
½ cup melted butter
½ cup minced onion

1 can cream of mushroom or celery soup
1 small carton sour cream
1 cup shredded cheddar cheese
Corn flake crumbs

Combine first 6 ingredients and stir well. Spoon into greased casserole. Sprinkle corn flake crumbs over potato mixture. Bake at 350 degrees for 30 minutes.

POLYNESIAN POTATOES

4 pounds whole potatoes, cooked and peeled
1 cup chopped onions
¼ cup butter
1 can condensed cream of celery soup

1 pint sour cream
2 cups shredded cheddar cheese
½ cup corn flake crumbs
3 T. melted butter

Prepare potatoes as above. Chill potatoes for 2-3 hours. Shred potatoes into bowl. Saute' onion in 1/4 cup butter until tender. Stir in soup and sour cream. Add cheese and mix well. Put into greased baking dish. Sprinkle with corn flake crumbs, and pour melted butter over top. Bake at 325 degrees for 1 hour.

CROCK POT POTATOES

Put 12 clean potatoes that have been well greased into crock pot. Cover and cook on low about 10 hours or until tender.

SOUR CREAM POTATO CASSEROLE

5-6 medium potatoes
1 teaspoon salt
1 cup sour cream
5-6 green onions, minced

1 cup shredded cheddar cheese
½ cup melted butter
Corn flake crumbs

Cook potatoes in boiling salted water until tender. Remove skins, cool and grate. Combine remaining ingredients with grated potatoes. Pour into greased casserole dish. Sprinkle with corn flake crumbs over top. Bake at 350 degrees for 30 minutes.

HOLLANDAISE POTATOES

2 dozen new small potatoes
½ t. salt
½ t. pepper
½ stick butter
¼ cup minced parsley

3 egg yolks
2 T. lemon juice
½ t. salt
1 stick melted butter

Cook potatoes in skins in boiling, salted water until tender. Dip potatoes in 1/2 stick melted butter. Sprinkle with salt, pepper and parsley.

Combine egg yolks, lemon juice, salt and melted butter. Beat on high speed until mixture is smooth. Pour over potatoes. Serve hot.

53

POTATO CHEESE PUFF

3 beaten egg yolks
¼ cup milk
3 cups mashed, seasoned potatoes

2 cups shredded cheese
1 t. onion
3 stiffly beaten egg whites

Combine egg yolks and milk. Add potatoes, cheese and onion, and beat well. Fold egg whites into mixture. Place in greased baking dish. Bake at 350 degrees for 40-50 minutes until a knife inserted in the center comes out clean.

CELERY POTATOES

5-6 medium potatoes
1 can cream of celery soup
Salt and pepper

½ soup can milk
1 small minced onion

Peel potatoes and slice. Place sliced potatoes in greased casserole dish. Top with minced onions. Sprinkle with salt and pepper. Mix soup and milk together and pour over potatoes. Cover and cook at 350 degrees for 40-50 minutes.

POTATO PUFFS

5 cups hot mashed potatoes
8 oz. soft cream cheese
1 beaten egg

1 t. salt
Dash of pepper

Blend together potatoes and cream cheese. Add egg, salt, and pepper and beat thoroughly. Put into buttered baking dish. Brush with melted butter and bake at 350 degrees for 45 minutes.

POTATO CHIP CASSEROLE

½ cup chopped onion
2 T. butter
2 T. bacon
1¼ cup milk

6 boiled eggs - sliced
1 cup potato chip crumbs
12 pieces of bacon, fried and crumbled
1 cup shredded cheddar cheese

Cook onion in butter, blend in flour and milk, stirring while cooking until mixture thickens. Add cheese and stir until cheese melts. Place layer of egg slices in greased baking dish. Cover with half the cheese sauce, half the potato chips, and half the bacon. Repeat this layer again. Bake for 30 minutes in a 350 degree oven.

APPLE-POTATO BAKE

*Blend first 2 ingredients together to make Lipton Onion Butter.

*1 envelope Lipton Onion Soup Mix
*8 oz. whipped butter
½ cup brown sugar
½ cup chopped pecans

1 t. ground cinnamon
4 cups sliced cooked sweet potatoes
3 cups sliced apples slightly cooked

Blend Lipton Onion Butter, sugar, pecans and cinnamon. In a greased baking dish, layer 1/3 potatoes and apples and onion butter mixture. Repeat again two times and top last layer with 2 tablespoons onion butter. Bake at 350 degrees for 30 minutes.

SWISS POTATOES

5 medium potatoes
½ stick melted butter
Dash of salt and pepper

1 cup shredded Swiss cheese
3 T. parmesan cheese

Peel, slice and cook potatoes in boiling, salted water until tender. Place in greased baking dish and sprinkle with salt and pepper. Top with melted butter and cheeses. Brown in 350 degree oven for about 15 minutes.

HAM STUFFED POTATOES

3 large potatoes
¼ pound shredded cheese
2 T. heavy cream
3 T. butter

1 cup chopped cooked ham
½ t. salt
½ t. pepper

Bake potatoes until done. Cut potatoes in half and scoop out insides. Mash potatoes with cheese, cream, butter, salt and pepper. Then stir in ham bits. Spoon mixture back into shells and place on cookie sheet. Sprinkle with grated Parmesan cheese. Bake in oven for 10 minutes at 400 degrees.

HOT POTATO PUFFS

2 cups cooked, mashed potatoes
1 cup flour
2 t. baking powder

2 beaten eggs
1 t. salt
¼ t. pepper

Mix together well all ingredients and chill for 1-2 hours. Drop by tablespoons into deep hot oil and cook until golden brown.

CORN CHOWDER-POTATOES

¼ pound salt pork
1 chopped medium onion
2 stalks celery
4 medium potatoes, cubed
2 cups water

2 cups corn (fresh or frozen)
4 cups milk
Salt and pepper
3 T. butter, melted

Cook salt pork in Dutch oven until crisp. Remove from drippings and drain. Saute' the onion and celery in the drippings until tender. Add the potatoes and water. Cover and cook until potatoes are tender. Add corn and milk. Simmer for 10-15 minutes uncovered. Add salt and pepper to desired taste. Stir in butter. Serve warm.

LEMON POTATOES

8 large potatoes
½ cup melted butter
1/3 cup lemon juice
3 t. salt
½ t. nutmeg, ground

½ t. pepper
1 medium chopped onion
½ cup whipping cream
½ cup shredded cheddar cheese

Cook potatoes in boiling, salted water until tender. Drain and cool. Peel potatoes and cube. Combine next 6 ingredients and mix together well. Add this to potatoes and toss gently. Place in greased casserole and top with whipped cream. Sprinkle with cheese. Bake at 350 degrees until browned.

PIMIENTO POTATOES

5-6 cups cooked, cubed potatoes
1 medium onion, minced
1 small jar pimientos, chopped
1 t. Worcestershire sauce

1 can cream of mushroom soup
½ pound grated cheddar cheese
1 t. salt

Cook potatoes and onion in boiling salted water about 15 minutes. Add pimientos and cook 5 minutes more. Drain water off. Mix together potatoes, pimientos, onion, cheese, soup, Worcestershire sauce and salt. Pour in buttered casserole dish and bake at 350 degrees for 45-50 minutes.

POTATO-PINEAPPLE BOATS

6 medium potatoes
1 small jar cheese spread

1 small can crushed pineapple
1 t. salt

Bake potatoes until done. Cut potatoes in half lengthwise. Scoop out potato and save the shell. Mash potatoes and blend in enough milk to make fluffy. Add cheese spread, pineapple and salt. Pile mixture into the potato shell. Place in baking dish and bake for 20 minutes at 325 degrees.

BAKED POTATO TOPPER

Whip 1/4 cup soft butter and 1 cup shredded cheese. Add 1/2 cup dairy sour cream and 2 tablespoons snipped green onion.

OR

Whip 8 ounce package cream cheese and 1/3 cup light cream until fluffly. Add 1 tablespoon snipped chives, 1½ teaspoon lemon juice, 1/2 tsp. garlic salt.

Pour over top of baked potato halved.

GREEN BEAN AND POTATO CASSEROLE

1-2 pounds green beans
6 slices bacon
1 medium onion, chopped
2-3 T. bacon drippings

3-4 medium potatoes, cubed
¼ cup butter
¼ cup parmesan cheese

Cook green beans in boiling, salted water until tender. Fry bacon until crisp. Saute' onions in bacon drippings. Put bacon, drippings and onions in with green beans. Add butter and potatoes and cook until potatoes are tender. Place in baking dish. Sprinkle with bacon crumbs and parmesan cheese. Bake for 15 minutes at 350 degrees. Serve warm.

CREAMED PEAS AND NEW POTATOES

15 new potatoes
1-1½ cups fresh peas
3 T. sliced green onion
4 t. butter or margarine

4 tsp. all-purpose flour
1 cup milk
Salt to taste

Scrub potatoes, cook in boiling, salted water 15-20 minutes.

Cook peas and onions in small amount of boiling salted water 8-15 minutes. Make a white sauce of butter, flour, salt and milk. Combine sauce and vegetables. Serves 4-6.

Breakfast Potatoes

POTATO PANCAKES

3 beaten eggs
1 T. flour
1 t. salt

4 large potatoes (shredded)
Salad oil

Add flour and salt to beaten eggs and beat until smooth. Add potatoes and mix well.

Spoon mixture into hot frying pan in which salad oil covers bottom of pan. Flatten slightly, and fry until slightly brown. Turn and brown on other side. Serve with applesauce or bacon.

CHEESE POTATO PANCAKES

2 pounds potatoes
½ stick butter
4 oz. shredded Mozzarella cheese

1 egg
Salt and pepper

Boil the potatoes until tender. Peel and mash with one egg, butter, salt and pepper. (Mash potatoes by hand.) Shape potatoes into patties and fill the centers with cheese. Add a little flour if potatoes are too soft to hold.

Cover the bottom of a frying pan with cooking oil and heat. Fry patties until they are brown on each side.

POTATO PANCAKES - II

2 cups mashed potatoes
1 T. flour
2 T. dry bread crumbs
1 T. milk

1 egg
1 small grated onion
Salt and pepper

Mix the above ingredients and season with salt and pepper. Fry like pancakes in vegetable oil until brown.

POTATO DOUGHNUTS

½ cup mashed potatoes
½ cup sugar
1 package active dry yeast
1 t. salt
¼ t. baking soda
¼ t. baking powder
¾ cup milk

¼ cup cooking oil
1 t. vanilla
1 beaten egg
2½ cups all-purpose flour
Cooking oil for deep frying
½ cup sugar
¼ t. cinnamon

Combine first 9 ingredients. Let stand in a warm place for 30 minutes. Add egg and enough of the flour to make a soft dough. Turn out onto a floured surface and knead smooth for about 5 minutes.

Place in greased bowl, turning once to grease the surface. Cover again and let rise in a warm place until double, about 40-50 minutes. Roll out on floured surface to 1/3 inch thickness. Cut with doughnut cutter. Let rise for about 30 minutes. Fry in deep hot oil 1-2 minutes or until lightly brown on both sides. Combine the 1/2 cup sugar and cinnamon. Shake or sprinkle doughnuts with cinnamon sugar mixture while doughnuts are warm. Makes 18.

POTATO AND ZUCCHINI OMELET

8 eggs
2 T. milk
1 t. salt
1/8 t. pepper
4 T. vegetable oil

1 onion
3 medium potatoes, peeled and grated
2 zucchini, thinly sliced
1 T. butter
½ cup Parmesan cheese, grated

Beat eggs, milk, salt and pepper in a bowl. Heat 3 T. oil in skillet. Add onion and potatoes and cook for 3 minutes. Stir into egg mixture.

Clean skillet. Add 1 T. oil to skillet and saute' zucchini until tender. Remove from skillet and clean pan.

Melt butter in skillet. Add egg-potato mixture and sprinkle with 1/2 the cheese. Top with zucchini and the remaining cheese.

Bake at 375 degrees for about 20 minutes (until knife comes clean when inserted in the center). Loosen around edges and slide onto plate — zucchini side up.

TATER TOT BACON BITES

Cook package of bacon until almost done. Bake Tater Tots according to directions on package. Cut slices of American cheese into 3 strips and wrap one strip of cheese around each hot Tater Tot. Wrap strip of bacon around the cheese and secure with toothpick. Broil the Taters, turning one time, until bacon is crisp.

POTATO OMELET

1 large potato
5 T. butter
6 eggs

1 t. salt
¼ t. pepper

Cook potato, peel and dice. Melt 1 tablespoon butter in pan and stir in diced potatoes. Beat eggs. Cut 3 tablespoons of the butter into small pieces and stir into eggs. Add salt and pepper.

Melt remaining butter in an omelet pan or skillet. Pour in the egg mixture.

When omelet has set up, flip one side over and then another. When cooked and browned thoroughly, take out of skillet.

HASH BROWNS-CHEESE

4 slices of bacon
1 package hash browns
1 t. salt
1½ cups water

½ cup shredded cheddar cheese
4 eggs
½ cup milk

Fry bacon, drain and save drippings. Stir in potatoes, salt and water. Cook potatoes, uncovered, until potatoes are lightly browned, turning when necessary. Sprinkle cheese over potatoes. Beat together eggs and milk and pour over potatoes. Cover and cook until done. Sprinkle bacon crumbs over the top and serve warm.

HOT POTATO CAKES

1 package hash browns
2 well beaten eggs
¼ cup milk
2 T. flour

1 t. salt
¼ t. pepper
1 small onion - minced

Let potatoes set in hot water for 5 minutes and then drain well. Mix together potatoes and remaining ingredients. Drop by heaping teaspoon onto a hot, greased griddle. Cook on each side until brown.

TATERS, BACON AND EGGS

4 medium size potatoes
1 pound bacon
2 medium onions

8 eggs, 2 T. cream
1 t. salt
½ t. pepper

Cook potatoes in boiling, salted water until tender. Cut into thin slices. Fry bacon until crisp and drain. Save drippings. Crumble bacon. Put 5 tablespoons bacon drippings back into skillet. Saute' onions until tender. Add potato slices and cook for 10-15 minutes while turning until potatoes are brown on both sides. Beat eggs in a large bowl. Add cream, salt and pepper and beat again. Add bacon bits and egg mixture to the potatoes. Cook over low heat for 8-10 minutes, stirring occasionally until eggs are set.

Breads

POTATO-WHEAT BREAD

1 medium potato, peeled and shredded
1½ cups buttermilk
2 packages active dry yeast
4 T. sugar

2 T. shortening
1 T. salt
3 cups all-purpose flour
3 cups whole wheat flour

Cook potato in buttermilk for 15 minutes, uncovered. Cool. Set aside 1/2 cup of this liquid. Mash the potato in the remaining liquid. Add warm water to make 2 cups potato mixture.

In a mixing bowl, soften yeast in the 1/2 cup liquid from cooking the potatoes. Add the potato mixture, sugar, shortening, and 1 T. salt and mix well. Stir in 2 cups white flour. Beat on low for 1/2 minute, scraping sides of bowl constantly. Beat 3 minutes, and let rise in warm place about 40-50 minutes or until double in size.

Stir dough down. Stir in whole wheat flour and enough of the rest of all-purpose flour to make a moderately stiff dough. Turn out onto floured surface and knead until smooth and elastic (10 mintes). Shape into a ball. Place in greased bowl. Cover. Let rise about 30-40 minutes, or until double. Punch down. Turn out onto floured surface. Divide in half. Cover. Let stand for 10 minutes. Shape each half into a round loaf.

Place loaves on a greased baking sheet. Cover and let rise until double. Bake for 30-35 minutes at 375 degrees.

POTATO BREAD

10 potatoes
1 stick butter, melted
2 onions, minced

3 stalks of celery, chopped
Salt and pepper
10 slices of bread

Cook peeled potatoes in boiling water. Chill until cool. Mash potatoes with butter, celery, onions, salt and pepper. Dampen bread slices and mix into the potato mixture. Put in greased casserole dish and bake for 35-45 minutes at 350 degrees.

Sweet Potatoes

SWEET POTATO PUDDING

1 cup milk
2 T. butter
2 T. sugar
½ t. salt
2 cups cooked mashed sweet potatoes

2 eggs separated
1 T. nutmeg
¼ cup raisins
¼ cup pecans
1 cup marshmallows or coconut

Scald milk, add butter, sugar and salt. Add this to mashed potatoes. Add beaten egg yolks, nutmeg, raisins and nuts. Then fold in stiff egg whites. Pour in buttered casserole dish. Sprinkle with miniature marshmallows or coconut. Put in oven at 325 degrees until marshmallows are melted.

APRICOT-SWEET POTATOES

6-8 medium sweet potatoes
1 cup brown sugar
1 T. cornstarch
½ t. salt
½ t. ground cinnamon

1 cup apricot nectar
½ cup hot water
1 T. grated orange rind
2 T. butter
½ cup chopped pecans

Cook sweet potatoes in boiling, salted water until tender. Drain, cool, and slice potatoes. Combine next 7 ingredients and bring to a boil, stirring constantly. Remove from heat and stir in butter and pecans. Pour sauce over potatoes. Bake at 325 degrees for 30 minutes.

SWEET POTATO PIE

6 medium sweet potatoes, cooked & mashed
½ cup soft butter
2 eggs beaten
¼ cup of sugar
1 cup brown sugar
½ t. ginger
½ t. cinnamon
½ t. nutmeg
½ t. cloves
½ cup milk
1 unbaked 9″ pie shell

Combine first 10 ingredients and mix well. Pour into pie shell. Bake at 350 degrees for 30-40 minutes. Serve with whip cream if desired.

SWEET POTATO SOUFFLE

2 cups sweet potatoes, cooked
½ cup sugar
½ cup brown sugar
1 t. vanilla
2 beaten eggs
2 T. butter
1 small can crushed pineapple
1 cup raisins

Topping:
1 stick butter, melted
1 cup brown sugar
½ cup flour
1 cup coconut
½ cup chopped nuts

Blend together potatoes and sugars. Add next 5 ingredients and mix well. Pour into buttered baking dish. Mix together ingredients for topping and pour over potato mixture. Bake at 325 degrees for 20-30 minutes until brown.

ORANGE-SWEET POTATO BAKE

4 medium sweet potatoes, peeled,
cooked and sliced
½ cup brown sugar
½ t. salt
1 T. cornstarch

1 cup orange juice
3 T. rum
½ cup chopped pecans
1 t. grated orange peel

Place potatoes in greased baking dish and sprinkle with salt. Combine next 4 ingredients in a saucepan and cook until boiling while stirring all the time. Add rum and pour over potatoes. Sprinkle with pecans and orange peel. Bake at 325 degrees for 30 minutes.

CANDIED SWEET POTATOES

½ cup flour
¾ cup packed brown sugar
½ cup oats, uncooked
1 t. cinnamon
1 t. cloves

1 stick butter
2 16 oz. can sweet potatoes or yams
2 cups cranberries
1 cup miniature marshmallows

Combine first 5 ingredients. Then cut in 1 stick butter until mixture is coarse. Mix 1 cup of the mixture with 2 cans whole sweet potatoes/yams and 2 cups cranberries. Put in casserole and top with remaining crumbly mixture. Bake at 350 degrees for 30 minutes. Then top with 1 cup marshmallows and put back into oven until marshmallows are lightly browned.

SWEET POTATO BISCUITS

1 cup all purpose flour
1 T. baking powder
½ t. salt

¼ cup butter, softened
1 large sweet potato, cooked and mashed
3-4 T. milk

Combine dry ingredients. Cut in butter and add mashed potatoes and enough milk to make a soft dough. Roll dough out on floured boarad. Cut with biscuit cutter and place on greased baking sheet. Bake at 425 degrees for about 15 minutes or until lightly browned.

SWEET POTATO KABOBS

Sweet potatoes
Pineapple chunks

Melted butter

Cook sweet potatoes in their skins until tender (about 30 minutes). Cool, slip off skins, and cut sweet potatoes into 1-inch cubes. Place potato cubes and pineapple on a skewer - alternating one and then another. Brush with melted butter. Place on grill and cook about 25-30 minutes or until brown.

PINEAPPLE YAMS

1 can yams or sweet potatoes
1 cup crushed pineapple with juice

1/3 cup flaked coconut

Place yams or sweet potatoes into casserole or baking pan. Cover with crushed pineapple and sprinkle with coconut. Cover with aluminum foil. Bake at 325 degrees for 40-45 minutes.

SWEET POTATOES AND FRANKS

1 20 oz. can pineapple chunks
1 18 oz. can sweet potatoes (halved)
1 pound frankfurters (cut in half)
½ cup packed brown sugar
2 T. chili sauce

2 T. cornstarch
½ cup orange juice
2 T. vinegar

Drain pineapple and save liquid. Arrange pineapple, sweet potatoes and frankfurters in baking dish. In saucepan, combine brown sugar and cornstarch. Stir in pineapple juice, orange juice, vinegar and chili sauce. Cook until thick and bubbly. Pour over mixture in baking dish. Cover and bake in a 350 degree oven for 30 minutes.

SWEET POTATOES AND PORK

2 cans pork luncheon meat
1 can sweet potatoes
½ cup corn syrup

½ cup orange juice
1 T. melted butter
1 jar spiced crab apples

Slice luncheon meat into slices and place in baking dish. Place sliced potatoes on top of meat slices. Combine corn syrup, orange juice and butter. Pour over meat and potatoes. Place crab apples on top and bake at 350 degrees for 30 minutes.

ALMOND SWEET POTATO PUFFS

3 cups mashed cooked sweet potatoes
3 T. melted butter
6 T. orange marmalade
2/3 cup chopped almonds

1 egg
½ t. salt

Combine mashed potatoes with melted butter, marmalade, egg and salt. Beat until smooth. Chill. Spread almonds on sheet of waxed paper. Drop potato mixture by large tablespoons onto almonds. Roll to coat on all sides. Shape into balls and place in greased baking dish. Bake at 400 degrees for 15 minutes.

HAWAIIAN SWEET POTATOES

2 cans sweet potatoes
1 8 oz. can crushed pineapple
1 stick butter, melted
½ cup sugar
1 t. cinnamon

1 t. cloves
½ cup pecans, chopped
½ cup brown sugar
½ stick butter

Drain pineapple and save syrup. Combine sweet potatoes, butter, sugars, cinnamon, cloves and drained pineapple. Beat thoroughly. Fold in pecans and 1/4 cup pineapple syrup. Place in buttered casserole dish. Sprinkle with butter. Bake at 350 degrees for 30 minutes.

SWEET POTATO BISCUITS

1 cup mashed sweet potatoes
4 T. melted butter
2/3 cup milk
1¼ cups flour

3½ t. baking powder
2 T. sugar
½ t. salt

Combine first 3 ingredients. Sift together next 4 ingredients, and add to sweet potato mixture. Turn out onto floured board. Toss lightly until dough looks smooth. Roll out to 1/2" thickness. Cut with biscuit cutter. Place on greased baking pan. Bake 15 minutes in 450 degree oven.

BOURBON YAMS

4-6 medium cooked yams, peeled and sliced
1 cup sugar
½ cup brown sugar

2 T. milk
4 oz. bourbon

Mash yams with sugars, milk and bourbon. Beat until fluffy. Pour into buttered casserole dish and top with marshmallows. Bake at 350 degrees for 15 minutes.

RUM-SWEET POTATOES

6 medium sweet potatoes, cooked and peeled
¼ cup melted butter
½ cup brown sugar

¼ cup rum
Dash of salt
½ cup chopped pecans

Combine first 5 ingredients, and beat until smooth. Pour into greased casserole dish and sprinkle with pecans. Bake at 325 degrees for 30-35 minutes.

SWEET POTATOES AND PINEAPPLE

1 can sweet potatoes
1 can sliced pineapple
½ cup brown sugar

2 T. butter, melted
Dash of salt

Place sweet potatoes in bottom of baking dish. Next, add drained pineapple slices. Combine 3 T. pineapple syrup, brown sugar, butter and dash of salt. Pour over potatoes and pineapple. Bake at 350 degrees for 15 minutes.

SWEET POTATO CASSEROLE

4 cups cooked sweet potatoes, sliced
1 stick butter, softened
1 cup sugar
Dash of salt

Topping: ¼ cup flour
1 cup crushed cornflakes

3 beaten eggs
1 t. vanilla
1 small can evaporated milk
½ cup brown sugar
1 cup chopped pecans

Mix together first 7 ingredients. Place in buttered baking dish. Mix together ingredients for the topping and sprinkle over potato mixture. Bake at 350 degress for 15 to 20 minutes.

SWEET POTATO PUDDING

2 cups grated sweet potatoes
1 cup sugar
3 eggs, beaten
Dash of salt
1 cup shredded coconut

1 t. cinnamon
1 t. vanilla
2 cups milk
½ stick melted butter

Mix together well all ingredients. Bake in buttered baking dish and bake at 375 degrees for 45 minutes.

CANDIED SWEET POTATOES

6 medium sweet potatoes
1 cup brown sugar
1 cup orange juice

1 lemon, squeezed
¼ cup butter or margarine, melted
1 t. cinnamon

Boil sweet potatoes until almost done. Peel and cut in cubes and place in buttered casserole dish. Combine remaining ingredients and pour over potatoes. Bake potatoes basting several times.

CROCK POT SWEET POTATOES

Place clean sweet potatoes in peelings along with 1/4 cup water in crock pot. Cover and cook for 1 hour on high. After 1 hour, turn to low for 8 hours or until tender.

ORANGE SWEET POTATOES

1 small package orange gelatin
¼ cup brown sugar
1 cup boiling water

4 T. butter
2 17 oz. cans sweet potatoes

Dissolve gelatin, brown sugar and a dash of salt in a skillet in boiling water. Add butter and while stirring constantly bring to a boil. Add sweet potatoes and simmer about 15 minutes until syrup thickens and potatoes are glazed.

SWEET POTATO-CRANBERRY BOATS

3 large sweet potatoes
½ cup cranberry-orange relish
¼ cup raisins
½ cup packed brown sugar

½ t. salt
3 T. butter
½ cup broken pecans

Cook sweet potatoes until tender in boiling salted water. Peel and cut in half lengthwise. Scoop out centers and save shells. Mix together potato pulp and relish and whip until fluffy. Stir in raisins and stuff back into shells. Combine sugar and salt and cut in butter. Stir in nuts. Sprinkle this mixture over potatoes. Bake in 325 degree oven about 30 minutes.

SWEET POTATO PUDDING

2 cups grated raw sweet potatoes
2 eggs
1 cup sugar
1 small can evaporated milk
½ cup milk

1 t. ground cinnamon
1 t. ground nutmeg
1 t. salt
1 cup melted butter

Combine eggs and sugar and beat well. Then stir in remaining ingredients. Pour into greased casserole dish. Bake at 350 degrees at 1 hour.

POTATO-PEACH PUFFS

2 cups mashed sweet potatoes
1 t. lemon juice
3 T. brown sugar
Sprinkle of salt

½ t. ground cloves
2 T. butter
6 canned peach halves

Blend together first 6 ingredients and whip until fluffy. Arrange peaches in greased baking dishes. Pile each with potato mixture and dot with butter. Bake in 350 degree oven about 30 minutes.

CANDIED SWEET POTATO TREATS

Cut 6 sweet potatoes, cooked and peeled in 1/2" slices. Layer potatoes in buttered 1½ quart casserole with 3/4 cups brown sugar, 1 tsp. salt, and 1/4 cup butter. Bake at 350 degrees about 30 minutes or until glazed. Add 1/2 cup miniature marshmallows last 5 minutes and brown lightly. Serves 6.

APRICOT-SWEET POTATOES

6-8 medium sweet potatoes
1 cup dried apricots
½ stick butter

2 eggs
1 t. salt
1 t. brown sugar

Cook sweet potatoes until tender. Drain and peel. Cook apricots in boiling water about 8-10 minutes. Beat sweet potatoes, apricots and butter until fluffy. Beat in eggs, salt and brown sugar. Put in greased casserole and bake for 1 hour at 325 degrees uncovered.

PINEAPPLE-SWEET POTATOES

5 or 6 medium sweet potatoes
1 cup sugar
½ t. salt
1 t. cinnamon
½ t. nutmeg

½ cup butter
3 beaten eggs
½ cup crushed pineapple
1½ cups milk
½ cup coconut (option)

Cook sweet potatoes until tender. Peel potatoes and mash. Add next 8 ingredients and mix well. Pour into a greased baking dish. Bake at 350 degrees for 45 minutes. Sprinkle with coconut if desired.

Desserts

POTATO CAKE

½ cup warm water
1 t. sugar
2 packages dry yeast
1 cup milk
½ cup sugar
½ cup shortening
1 t. salt
1 cup mashed cooked potatoes

2 lightly beaten eggs
6 cups all-purpose flour
1 stick soft butter
1 cup raisins
½ cup chopped pecans
1 cup sugar
1 t. cinnamon
1 egg white, beaten

Combine very warm water, 1 t. sugar and yeast. Let stand for 10-12 minutes in a warm place. Mix together next 6 ingredients. Add to yeast. Gradually add flour until well blended. Add remaining ingredients. Pour into floured, greased bundt pan. Bake at 325 degrees until done.

POTATO CHIP COOKIES

1 cup white sugar
1 cup brown sugar
1 cup shortening
2 eggs
1 tsp. vanilla

2 cups self-rising flour
2 cups oatmeal
1 cup pecans
2 cups crushed potato chips

Cream together first 3 ingredients. Add eggs and vanilla and blend well. Add flour gradually. Stir in last 3 ingredients. Drop by teaspoons onto greased cookie sheet. Bake for 10-12 minutes at 375 degrees.

SWEET POTATO ICE CREAM

3 quarts vanilla ice cream
2 17 oz. cans mashed sweet potatoes

½ cup lemon drop candy - crushed

Let ice cream soften at room temperature. Stir in mashed sweet potatoes. Cover and chill around 5 hours. Pour into 5-quart ice cream freezer and freeze according to freezer directions. Add crushed lemon candy when ice cream is almost frozen.

COCONUT POTATO CANDY

¾ cup cold mashed potatoes
(nothing added)
4 cups confectioners sugar

4 cups flaked coconut
1½ t. vanilla
½ t. salt

Combine all ingredients and blend well. Drop by teaspoons on waxed paper.

POTATO CANDY

¼ cup warm mashed potatoes
1 t. melted butter
1¾ cups powdered sugar

1½ cups coconut (flaked)
½ t. vanilla

Combine potatoes and butter in a bowl. Add sugar gradually and beat until blended. Add remaining ingredients and mix well. Drop by teaspoon onto waxed paper and let stand until firm.

INDEX

Main Dish Potatoes

Potato Meat Roll	2
Potato-Cheeseburger Casserole	2
Hamburger-Potato Pie	3
Potato-Ham Mold	3
Baked Ham & Potatoes	4
Baked Hot Dog-Wieners	4
Potato Stew	5
Baked Potato Stew	5
Meat Balls & Potatoes	6
Sausage & Potatoes	6
Ham-Potato Hash	7
Sweet Potato-Pork Chop Casserole	7
Pork Chops-Potato Casserole	8
Potatoes and Chops	8
Fish Balls	8
Shrimp Potatoes	9
Scallops-Potatoes	9
Potato-Tuna Pie	10
Taters and Fish	10
Skillet Steak and Potatoes	11
New England Beef & Potatoes	11
Potato Hash	12
Potato-Polish Sausage Casserole	12
Potatoes and Beef	13
Potato Pizza	13
Skillet Potatoes and Ham	14
Potato-Taco Pie	14
Ham and Potato Loaf	15
Bratwurst and Potatoes	15
Chicken Gratin Potatoes	16
Ham Hocks and Potatoes	16
Rabbit-Potatoes Stew	17

Hot & Cold Potato Salads

Chicken-Potato Salad	19
Shoestring Potato-Meat Salad	19
Potato Salad With Chicken and Ham	20
German Potato Salad	20
Vegetable Salad	21
Chicken-Potato Salad II	21
Ham-Potato Salad	22
Meat-Potato Salad	22
Cheese-Potato Salad	23
Bean-Potato Salad	23

Potato-Hot Dog Salad	24
Creamy Potato Salad	24
Meat-Potato Salad II	25
Sour Cream -Potato Salad	25
Corned Beef and Potato Salad	26
Hot Potato Salad	26
Italian Potato Salad	26
Sausage-Potato Salad	27
Hot Potato Salad II	27
Bean Potato Salad	28
Dill Potato Salad	28
Dill-Potato Salad II	29
Green Pepper Potato Salad	29
Hot Potato Salad	30
Sour Cream Potato Salad	30
Potato Salad	31
Potato Salad-Scalloped	31
Potato-Sardine Salad	32
Hot German Potato Salad	32
Potato and Corned Beef-Salad	33
Apple-Potato Salad	33
Parmesan Potato Salad	34
Potato Salad With Cottage Cheese	34
Skewered Potatoes	34
Potato-Spinach Salad	35
Potato Salad II	35
Garden Potato Salad	35
Potato Salad With Sour Cream	36
Salami-Potato Salad	36

Soups & Chowders

Potato Seafood Chowder	38
New England Clam Chowder	38
Potato Potage	39
Potato Chowder	39
Potato-Tomato Soup	40
Cream of Potato Soup	40
Potato Soup	40
Potato Soup	41
Cream of Potato Soup II	41

Hot Potatoes

Cheesed Spuds	43
Hot Potatoes	43
Volcano Potatoes	43
Scalloped Potatoes With Pimiento	44
Scalloped Potatoes	44
Double Potato Bake	45
Grilled Lemon Potatoes	45
Hot Deviled Potatoes	46
Potato Croquettes	46
Gold Ol' Mashed Potatoes	46
Grilled Potatoes	47
Potatoes and Peas	47
Grilled Onions-Potatoes	48
Barbecued Potatoes	48
Celery and Cheese Potatoes	49
Mustard Potatoes	49

Stuffed Potatoes 50
Mushroom Potatoes 50
Sesame Potatoes 51
Shrimp Potatoes 51
Cheese Potatoes 51
Hash Brown Potato Casserole 52
Polynesian Potatoes 52
Crock Pot Potatoes 52
Sour Cream Potato Casserole 53
Hollandaise Potatoes 53
Potato Cheese Puff 54
Celery Potatoes 54
Potato Puffs 54
Potato Chip Casserole 55
Apple-Potato Bake 55
Swiss Potatoes 56
Ham Stuffed Potatoes 56
Hot Potato Puffs 56
Corn Chowder-Potatoes 57
Lemon Potatoes 57
Pimiento Potatoes 58
Potato-Pineapple Boats 58
Baked Potato Topper 58
Green Bean and Potato Casserole 59
Creamed Peas and New Potatoes 59

Breakfast Potatoes

Potato Pancakes 61
Cheese Potato Pancakes 61
Potato Pancakes II 62
Potato Doughnuts 62
Potato and Zucchini Omelet 63
Tater Tot Bacon Bites 63
Potato Omelet 64
Hash Browns-Cheese 64
Hot Potato Cakes 65
Taters, Bacon and Eggs 65

Breads

Potato-Wheat Bread 67
Potato Bread 68

Sweet Potatoes

Sweet Potato Pudding 70
Aprico-Sweet Potatoes 70
Sweet Potato Pie 71
Sweet Potato Souffle 71
Orange-Sweet Potato Bake 72
Candied Sweet Potatoes 72

Sweet Potato Biscuits 73
Sweet Potato Kabobs 73
Pineapple Yams 73
Sweet Potatoes and Franks 74
Sweet Potatoes and Pork 74
Almond Sweet Potato Puffs 75
Hawaiian Sweet Potatoes 75
Sweet Potato Biscuits 76
Bourbon Yams 76
Rum-Sweet Potatoes 76
Sweet Potatoes and Pineapple 77
Sweet Potato Casserole 77
Sweet Potato Pudding 78
Candied Sweet Potatoes 78
Crock Pot Sweet Potatoes 78

Orange Sweet Potatoes 79
Sweet Potato-Cranberry Boats 79
Sweet Potato Pudding 80
Potato-Peach Puffs 80
Candied Sweet Potato Treats 80
Apricot-Sweet Potatoes 81
Pineapple Sweet Potatoes 81

Desserts
Potato Cake 83
Potato Chip Cookies 83
Sweet Potato Ice Cream 84
Coconut Potato Candy 84
Potato Candy 84